Counting

This math series is dedicated to Nick, Tony, Riley, and Hailey.

Published by The Child's World®
PO Box 326
Chanhassen, MN 55317-0326
800-599-READ
www.childsworld.com

Design and Production: The Creative Spark, San Juan Capistrano, CA
Photos: © David M. Budd Photography

Library of Congress Cataloging-in-Publication Data
Pistoia, Sara.
  Counting / by Sara Pistoia.
      p. cm. — (Mighty math series) (Easy reader)
Summary: Simple text describes the basics of counting and explains how
to count in groups.
  ISBN 1-56766-114-9 (lib. bdg. : alk. paper)
  1. Counting—Juvenile literature. [1. Counting.] I. Title. II.
Series. III. Easy reader (Child's World (Firm))
  QA113 .P564 2002
  513.2'11—dc21
                                                    2002004944

MIGHTY MATH

Counting

Sara Pistoia

The Child's World®

Why do we count? Sometimes we want to know how many of something there are. We could guess how many children are in this class. It looks as if there are a few—perhaps seven or eight.

If we want to know exactly how many children there are, we can count them!

If there aren't very many things to count, we can count by ones.

Hi! I'm Math Mutt! I counted four plus three more. There are exactly seven kids. If there are fewer than ten things, it's easy to count by ones.

Look at all the geese! It looks
as if there are more than ten!
Let's count by fives to see how
many geese there are.

How many groups of five are there? Could all of the geese fit into groups of five? We need to count by fives first. Then we count the rest by ones.

I counted two groups of five geese. There are two geese left over. Two groups of five make ten, plus two more. There are twelve geese walking on the grass!

How could we count all these buttons? We could count them by ones. But we can count them more quickly if we group them into piles of five.

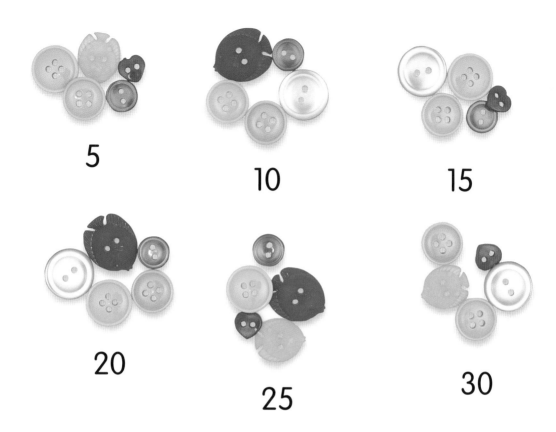

5

10

15

20

25

30

Now count by fives as you point to each pile.

Counting by fives is quick! Is there an even quicker way to count?

Now try counting the buttons by tens. First, group the buttons into piles of ten.

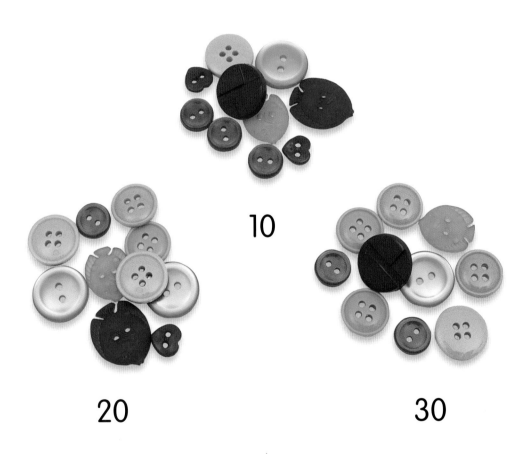

10

20

30

Did you count three piles of ten?
Good!

When you counted by fives, you
pointed to six piles. Remember?
But when you counted by tens,
you pointed to just three piles.

I see three piles of ten.
That's the same as thirty!

Look at this pile of rocks.
What's the best way to count
them? If you said by tens,
you're right!

First, sort the rocks into groups
of ten. Are there some left
over? Let's set those aside
and count them last. We'll
count them by ones.

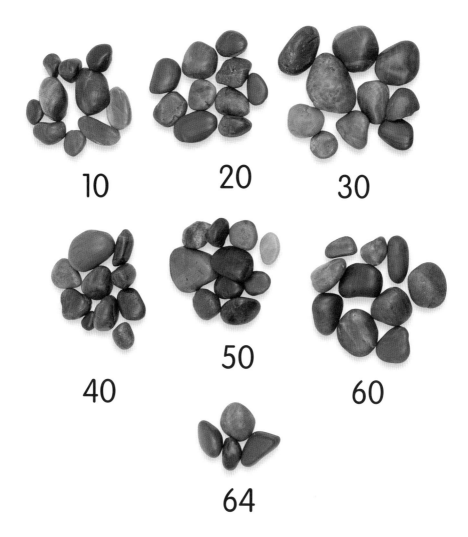

10

20

30

40

50

60

64

I counted to sixty by tens. Then I counted four
extra rocks by ones. That equals sixty-four rocks.

60 + 4 = 64

13

How can we write the amount using numerals instead of words? We'll have to remember which numeral shows how many tens we have. And we'll have to remember which numeral shows how many ones we have.

We write the number of tens on the left. We write the number of ones on the right. Each number has its own place value.

tens	ones
6	4

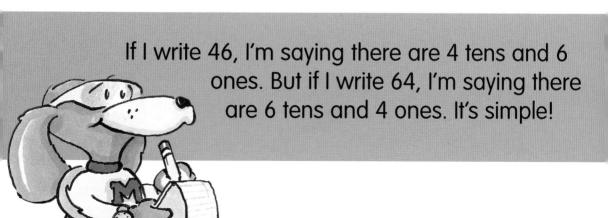

If I write 46, I'm saying there are 4 tens and 6 ones. But if I write 64, I'm saying there are 6 tens and 4 ones. It's simple!

Do you like jelly beans?
Which bag would you choose?

14   41

I want to share my jelly beans.
I'll need a lot! I'll take the bag
with forty-one jelly beans.

16

What if you choose the bag with fourteen (14) jelly beans? You'll get one group of ten plus four more jelly beans.

What if you choose the bag with forty-one (41) jelly beans? You'll get four groups of ten jelly beans, plus one extra!

tens	ones
4	1

If you get both bags of jelly beans, how many do you have?

You can add the numbers and find out. You can add them just as the picture shows.

First, let's add ones to ones. Then let's add tens to tens.

tens	ones
4	1
+ 1	4
5	5

19

Wow! This bag holds a lot of peanuts! What if you counted ninety-nine (99) peanuts plus one more? You would need another special number. One hundred!

To write one hundred, we add a number to the left of the tens. When you count this many things, you really have to keep track!

hundreds	tens	ones
1	0	0

Remember to put the numbers in their special places: ones, tens, and hundreds.

How many books are there?
Count them!

How many kittens are there?
Count them!

You can count by ones, by fives, and by tens. And you can keep track of how many things you count. Just be sure to write the numbers in their special places.

That's enough math for today.
Let's play with the kittens!

Key Words

amount

count

equal

fives

hundreds

numeral

ones

place value

tens

Index

About the Author

Sara Pistoia is a retired elementary teacher living in Southern California with her husband and a variety of pets. After 40 years of teaching, she now contributes to education by supervising and training student teachers at California State University at Fullerton. In authoring this series, she draws on the experience of many years of teaching first and second graders.